CAT LINES

An anthology of cat poems
edited by Alison Chisholm

CAT LINES

EL CAPITÁN animal project e.V. is a welfare organisation that cares for stray and feral cats on the Canary Island of Fuerteventura. It helps prevent animal suffering by addressing the stray cat population with neutering; and tries to offer a better way of life for the existing stray cats, from setting up and maintaining Cat Feeding Stations to emergency veterinary care. El Capitán also works to encourage the adoption of abandoned cats and create a better understanding of cats among the island's inhabitants.

When a cat has been treated, the tip of its left ear is removed. So if you see a lopsided feline face, you can be sure that the cat is known and cared for by a team of dedicated volunteers - assisted by you, through your purchase of this book, and also by the poets who have generously donated their work for inclusion.

EL CAPITÁN animal project e.V.
Lichtenbroicher Weg 8a, 40472 Dusseldorf.
Registerblatt VR 9650, Steuernummer: 105/5895/1366
www.animal-project.de

Dedicated to the memory of Orlando – a Cat with Attitude.

ISBN 978-1-4467-0235-2

First published by lulu.com, 2010.

THE CREATURE

When midnight arrives and the silence has begun,
the pace of the creature is a fast, racing one.

When the cold winds blow and the werewolves howl
the shadow of the creature gives a loud yowl.

Tall, slender, wise and proud,
it likes to be alone and not in a crowd.

It dances in the moonlight and leaps off the ground,
then crouches silent, and doesn't make a sound.

It sleeps all day and curls up on the mat.
If you haven't guessed yet, yes, it's a cat.

Jessica Shortland

CAT HAT

Mrs. Maguire,
as blind as a bat,
put her cat on her head
and patted her hat.

To her surprise
when out shopping that day,
a dog gave a bark
and her hat ran away.

Denise Randall

FRIED MOUSE ANYONE?

I love Anna, she is kind.
She feeds me fish and bacon rind,
Meat and tasty bits of cheese,
So I do my best to please.

I've purrfect manners, like most cats.
I wash my paws and spotless spats,
And only scratch the new settee
Where it's difficult to see.

I once brought in a fine fat mouse …
But Anna's screams rang through the house.
She pushed me right outside the door,
So I thought, 'That mouse was raw …

Perhaps she'd like it cooked instead,
Go nicely with some crusty bread.'
So next time, in the frying pan,
I slid a mouse beside the ham.

I thought it made a tasty treat,
But had to make a swift retreat,
As Anna flung pan, ham and mouse
Into the yard behind the house.

I couldn't let it go to waste,
And Twinkles, you'd have loved the taste.

Shirley Tomlinson

HOME TO HOME
(In memory of Queenie)

If it's loyalty you're after
I'm not the best of pets.
I need to spread myself around
I need to hedge my bets.

For coley, cod or kippers
it's number forty-two.
I visit Wednesday mornings
when the fishmonger is due.

In number twenty's garden
I settle in the sun,
nap for a couple of hours
then mug some mice for fun.

When it's cold and rainy
there's a man who lives alone;
I have to guard his duvet
when he works away from home.

One couple think they own me;
- catflaps don't prove a thing –
but I know I'll raid their pantry
when my kittens come this spring.

Sandra Burnett

SPEEDY CAT

Fat and black,
fur long and knotty,
face flat,
generally grotty,
a shoddy moggy!

Catcher supreme,
ugly extreme,
in Tessier Gardens crouched,
lumpishly leans,
malicious and mean,
a one eyed bandit machine!

He chases all the squirrels,
clawing at their tails,
across the winding trails,
along the wooden rails
with herbs writ up in Braille;
to gazebo filigreed and frail
until the mulberries are scaled.

'Ay he's faster than he seems,
Speedy that cat.'

Lucinda Carey

BREAK A PAW DARLING

You may call me Sophia
but never Sophia the Siamese.
As an accomplished actress

I find such alliteration so passé.
Well, I say actress –
I don't bother much these days.
I'm not exactly retired –
I potter in the garden,
read a little Eliot, I'm as we felines
call it, resting and reflecting.
Of course you'll remember me
from such films as 'A Streetcat named Desire,'
'The Sound of Mewing' and 'Kitten Kong.'
I nearly became a Bond Girl,
only that obese bag of pallid fur,
Madame Blankski, was the one
who got to sleep on Blofeld's knee.
I believe in forgive and forget –
by the way she wears a wig.
Not that I'm bitter, no, I went on to marry
Romeo, my seventh husband,
took time out to raise a couple of litters.
Of course, as you will know,
I'm now heavily involved
in a sponsorship deal with a company
called 'Kitty Dinners.'
I don't actually eat the revolting stuff,
the smell alone is enough to put one off,
but it does pay the rent on our small basket
in Tuscany. Anyway must go darlings
I'm expecting a call from that lovely Mr. Webber;
a cat playing a human playing a cat, how clever.

Stephen Beattie

A KENNING FOR KITTY

paw dangler
fish pond angler

bird stalker
tightrope walker

fine diner
mouse diviner

fur licker
city slicker

vase breaker
mischief maker

caterwauler
back yard brawler

bed warmer
nessun dorma!

Jayne Stanton

TILLY MINT'S SONNET

That Paul's all right. It's her I can't abide.
She's maladroit, she frightens me, her voice
is shrill – a peacock's scream. I've tried and tried
to rub along, without success. I'm choiceless,
'cos I can't move out. Where would I go?
To bare Bleakholt, the house where I was born?
They called me Dopey, a gnome's name. So, no
I can't go back. She knows I'm just a pawn
in the great game of life. Alas! But when
the lights go out, I jump up on their bed
Miaow! Miaow! I turn comedienne
become a brave, emboldened quadruped.

She rolls me on my back. I don't get frickled
and, ecstasy, I have my tummy tickled.

Jean Tarry

LITTERMATES HAIKU

Byron and Shelley,
ginger and tabby couplet,
purr pentameters.

Alison Chisholm

TIGGY

Soft gentle cat purring and blinking,
is it of cream and a fireside you're thinking
with tightly closed eyes that seemingly smile,
or is it quite simply you're resting a while?

Soft gentle cat, what are you watching?
Toad or grasshopper there for the swotting?
Soppy with sleep you hardly can care;
of spoils you well know you'll get your fair share.

Round golden eyes, alert, wide awake,
sharp claws are spread to toss and to shake.
Those paws whilst you slept looked so furry and gentle,
but those talons of yours are not incidental.

I gather you up all bristling and wild,
and comfort and soothe you just like a child.
Darling luxurious funny old cat
doze, my sweet Tiggy, upon your warm mat.

Chrystal Tuckfield.

HOUSEHOLD

Their cat is the colour of coal;
coolly shining,
his is the best grade
of this primeval substance.

In every other respect,
he's like flame:
he flows through any hold
had over him,

flicks a trance-like dance
over books and a precarious
pile of mail, plus twenty nine
steps of anniversary gifts.

From the man to the woman:
beads, embroidered cotton
and a delicate filigree leaf,
while from woman to man:

swiss army tools,
miniature compass, torch
with integral spirit level.
None of these things a cat needs;

he knows his balance,
even in darkness, is perfect,
as is his sense of direction
and beauty, unadorned.

A long way into the night,
he will sneak up to wake his couple
by stroking himself
on their feet, sticking out

from the end of the bed.
It's Dartmoor
and time to complain
in a treble, about the rain.

Susan Taylor

ELEGY

I miss him in the morning
when he'd pester me awake,
I miss him in the evening
when I always had to take
the dog out for her last walk
and he would come with us,
crossing the prom with cunning,
a very streetwise puss.
I miss him when I'm working,
this cat adored PCs,
he'd issue strange instructions
with his paws upon the keys.
And when I do the crossword
I miss the way he'd sit
right on the clues to stop me
trying to finish it.
Death may now have claimed him,
but it cannot claim the store
of memories we amass with time
from pets that we adore.

Peggy Poole

CELIA

Celia squirms, poor seasick cat:
- O catamaran, O catamaran -
Her eyes are wide and her ears are flat;
her fur's an unbrushed, tangled mat
and going to sea was a terrible plan
     for the waves are very wet.

Celia longs to be standing still,
- O catamaran, O catamaran -
or searching the garden for mice to kill,
or finding the sun on a windowsill.
She's being as brave as she possibly can
     but she can't see dry land yet.

Celia wails. She's tired and thin.
- O catamaran, O catamaran -
The Captain shouts, 'Cat! Stop that din!
This harbour's home. We're sailing in.'
She leaps for the shoreline, as fast as she can;
     it's a trip she won't forget.

Now Celia never goes to sea.
- O catamaran, O catamaran -
She sleeps in the garden, she hides in a tree.
She only sees fishes to eat them for tea
     in a mackerel baguette.

Margaret Richens

WOKEN UP!

Tabby cat curled asleep.
Won't be got up!

Warm in the duvet,
   in her soft velvet jacket,
she clings with her claws,

snarls, and waves her tail
   to question mark the morning.

Very cross puss, unpursuadable,
   but adorably leggy;
feline necked and pointy chinned.

Lucinda Carey

NEW HOME

When my parents moved to a flat
The neighbours waved, goodbye kissing.
One week later, guess who had gone?
Frantic phone calls, 'Our cat's missing!'

Dad went to check the old front garden,
Searched around for hours and hours;
Something cracks and shakes the bracken.
Guess who's hiding in the flowers?

They kept that cat locked up three weeks
They couldn't let him roam alone
Until at last he settled in
Happily in their brand new home.

Angela Lansbury

LOST AND FOUND

Black and white
first child
satisfied
my maternal instincts
for a while.

She played
with a poodle up the road
filled our house with interest
but one day she failed
to come home.

Two weeks passed
full of sunshine
outside,
but dull indoors
as we tried not to decide.

And then one day, in the drive,
I found a strange, grey,
half-drowned rodent;
skin not fur.
It was her!

She dragged herself up the stairs,
trembled for three weeks,
relived her escape.
One down,
she still has eight.

Anne Watson

WHAT CREEPS IN THE NIGHT?

Black Bertha creeps up to the window
Peers into the house, is he there?
Harry watches from the top of the stairs
Not today lady, not today he swears

Today he is king of his corner,
His green grape eyes flash, she waits poised
Big Bertha's mane gleams silk in the sunlight
A movement with his paw, whoosh she takes flight.

Licks her shirtfront, black like a mineshaft
Unsure of strategy, action
Watches the house from the dense hawthorn hedge
Sleep little one on your carpeted ledge

The moon laughs, gleams goodbye to the sun
Black Bertha prowls on silent paws
To the window, she heaves at the catdoor
A leap and feet skid on the marbled floor

Harry the Cat snores soundly, roundly
The black furball, low to the ground
Slithers to the richness, smell of the sea
'So sorry my dear, this is meant for me'

Diane Paul

THE LANGUAGE BARRIER

I call this my favourite chair.
You say it's a lap.
I call this my own front door.
You say it's a flap.

I call this my en-suite loo.
You say litter tray.
I call this your wake-up call.
You mumble, 'Go away!'

I call this my scratching post.
You say it's the stairs.
I call this shedding excess fur.
You bellow, 'Bloody hairs!'

I tell you that it's dinner time.
You pretend you haven't heard.
So I bring home a take-away
And you scream, 'It's a bird!'

I call this an outstretched paw.
You say laddered tights.
I call this my party trick.
You shout, 'Mind the lights!'

I call myself your closest friend.
You say I'm just a pet.
I call all night to attract a mate.
You drive me to the vet.

I call this a liberty.
You get me micro-chipped.
I call you lots of naughty words,
Then I end up getting snipped.

I've tried my best to talk to you.
I've miaowed and purred and spat.
But I'll never master Owner-speak
And you clearly don't speak Cat.

Vivien Hampshire

HUNTER

Dark ears above long grass.
Hunkered down,
the kitchen cat
pretends to be a fox.

Gwyneth Box

DISTINGUISHED VISITOR

In the year Twelve Hundred and Forty
When Hugh de Pateshall became Bishop of Lichfield,
The congregation, packed tightly together,
Were not expecting what would soon be revealed.

Chapels, choir-stalls, cloisters and altar
Were resplendent in red, blue and gold,
With a towering pulpit, ornately carved,
From which many an hour-long sermon was told.

As legend would have it, on the appointed day
Flares and candles lighted up the Cathedral.
Tension grew as congregation waited;
An air of restlessness filled the great hall.

Trumpets were raised to the heralds' lips,
Who blew a fanfare with mighty endeavour.
Rafters and pillars all shook with the sound,
Rending the air asunder.

On this grand occasion of Bishop Hugh's enthronement,
And all gathered filled with wonder and awe,
The great West Door of the Cathedral creaked open
And all gasped at what they saw.

No Bishop de Pateshall did they see,
No robes or ceremonial hat,
For as eyes scanned the doorway for a glimpse of Sir Hugh,
In sauntered … the Cathedral Cat!

With tail raised high in haughty deportment
Not once did his confidence falter.
He strutted the aisle with an air of occasion,
And laid his mouse down before the altar.

When you enter the Cathedral via the West Door,
Turn left into the Chapterhouse,
You'll see Cathedral Cat sculpted with Deans and monks,
Still smiling and clutching a mouse.

Dea Costelloe

ROBINSON

She sensed our weakness
that first frozen Friday,
when she wailed
at our door.

She enslaved us
as her willing pets,
gave purpose
to our lives.

The vet would only say,
'She has an excellent tail!'

Anne Watson

IF YOU WERE MINE

Me   by
nature
I'm a feral cat,
an independent feline
with a penchant for the wild
but I've decided to adopt
you, as you seem
to need
the company
and I can see from your
demeanour that you truly are
beguiled. I'd like salmon for my supper
and, for breakfast, full fat cream; a chaise
longue in the sunshine where I'd take a nap and
dream of diamond studded dishes piled high with
delicious kitty treats, and then party till I'm fit to
drop – my social life's my own – and, when I've   s
had enough of that and time to wander   t
home, I'd snuggle down beside you   e
on your   perfect   e
s   h
a   s
t i n

Denise Randall

DIPTYCH CATS

Now the vicar has retired
they're adjusting;
no bedroom each;

tabby islands on the carpet
Meg - unblinking moon-green eyes
Millie - creamy socks, cravat.

Aligned they face the same direction
or bookend, stare each other out.

Off ground pirates;
chair to table lightly winding

round the tea-cups, book-case bound,
flouncing on and off the Bible,

sniffing lamps and brushing flowers.
Nosing lap-wards onto papers

keyboard springboard, tread delete.
Bad cats, darlings, wicked pair

come and see what's in your dishes,
side by side, Meg here, Millie,
- greedy Millie - there!

Gail Mosley

CATS' DANCE

It was the night, the sparkling night, of the Cats' Annual Dinner and Ball
And any cat who was anybody made their way to the brightly lit hall.

Food and drink groaned on the tables, cocktails and tasty dishes piled high
And as society cats sashayed in, each breathed out a long pleasurable sigh.

Deep crusted mice pies, decorated with the most alluring pink tails
And golden fried spiders' legs clustered in delicate silver pails.

But first things first: no feline would want to be thought rude
Prizes had to be given before any could devour the food.

Each cat sat on a crimson seat and gracefully held their paws
And grudgingly prepared to give those who had won, a smattering of applause.

The first prize was for best mouser and it was no surprise it was Ali,
He had killed four hundred and twenty two, a most amazing tally.

The second prize was for fastest sprint, usually a hotly disputed claim
Bu all agreed that Lucky's whizzing speed was deserving of very wide fame.

And now a hush descended upon the Hall, the ladies sat up straight

For this was The Prize, the one that, for them, carried most weight

Yes,   every female cat, desperately and longingly aspired to this
It didn't matter a jot if she was a granny, a matron or a miss.

Although each cat smiled, each heart would count it as treason
If she did not carry off the awards for best dressed cat of the season

Would it be Cauliflower for hats decorated with the teeth of mice
Or Lucky with her striped berets, colourful, simple and nice.

Zoe cat wiggled on her chair doing the best she could to look demure
But surely the judges must be blind if they couldn't see the diamonds threaded in her fur.

Daisy had put her faith in sequins, when she moved her fur was aglow
And Dustee had encased her paws in bootees, the colour of pure white snow.

At last, Tom Cat, for it was he who judged, stood on his paws to declare
That there wasn't just one winner, instead all were entitled to share.

The ladies congratulated each other, and all gave their sweetest smiles
But at the end of the ball and all had gone home, Tom Cat was found pinned to the tiles.

Mairead Mahon

AGAINST ALL ODDS

She crept into his room, her usual style
Not to disturb him unnecessarily
      Or to provoke.

She'd learnt over many years how easy that was to do.
'An unlikely relationship that will not work,
      A miss-match,' it was said.

But standing beside his bed, her desire was overwhelming
To snuggle in beside him, caress the warmth
      Of his body against hers,

Feel again the comfort found in togetherness.
Old age had mellowed both, from fiery outbursts of youth,
      The endurance of middle-age truces,

To genial companionship
Of advancing years.
      Tentatively she eyed his lie,

Prone body relaxed in slumber.
Deafness now delayed his reactions.
      Stealthily she manoeuvred

Her sleek frame, with minimum disturbance.
He stirred at their contact,
      Black body against white.

A muffled grumble echoed as he moved
On to his side. She eased herself
      Into the contours of his warm body,

Relaxing, the arch of her back nestling
into the curve of his belly, revelling in contentment

That surrounded them,

He an old spaniel from a rescue home,
She a nineteen year old moggy
        From Manchester's Moss Side.

Dea Costelloe

AN ORNAMENTAL CAT

I sit on a dresser
looking disgruntled;
- can't change my expression
even if I wanted to.

My mistress – a failing witch –
couldn't get work.
I was no longer affordable
so, a quick spell and I became pot!

It was a simple solution for her.
She doesn't need to feed me,
but I find a sedentary life so boring.
I want to battle cats I deem inferior,

chase them through woods at night,
feel excitement coursing
through my veins again
as I clear the house of mice.

I wait, frustrated, for a reversal spell.

Dylys Osborne

FRED'S FANCY

If only Hallam had the sense,
He wouldn't crouch beneath the fence
Where all the birds just cannot fail
To catch the flick of his light tail.

With raucous cries they scoff and jeer
Since none of them have need to fear.
If only Hallam had the gall
And thought it through, he'd have them all.

Now Fred next door he'd got it sussed,
That ginger cat so sleek and brushed.
With confidence he ruled the block,
No bird dare look at him and mock.

And so it was there came a day
Fred hid himself beneath some hay.
A family of mice he'd spotted -
He knew he'd have one - or so he plotted.

But as with schemes of mice and men,
There came a rude awakening.
Fred found he'd hidden on a trailer
And was driven off – oh, what a failure!

So Hallam triumphed in the end,
The tabby cat who'd had no friend.
The birds are happy, the mice are safe -
And Fred's in hiding - the shame too great.

Lindsay Trenholme

WHAT'S IN A NAME?

I've settled in, the flat looks fine,
that comfy armchair I'll make mine,

but now I'm waiting patiently
to hear the name she'll choose for me.

She has 'The Works of William S'
so she'll pick something grand I guess.

Sebastian? Cornelius?
Vincentio? Demetrius?

She strokes my coat, I strike a pose,
head held high, green eyes composed.

I weave between her sandalled feet.
She offers tuna, what a treat.

I purr and think I'll take a bite,
but then I lose my appetite.

Crestfallen, I blink back the tears
for I cannot believe my ears –

me a handsome, cultured lion –
did she just say, 'Grub's up Brian!'

Denise Randall

TAMMY

She was very beautiful
and well aware of that.
She groomed her gorgeous stripey fur
and then she'd take a nap.
Do not disturb, be aware of that.

Her amber eyes were wonderful,
expressive, without fear.
She moved about with elegance,
aloof, yet well aware –
and no dog would ever dare.

Yet she was not beyond
an adventure in the night.
She could disappear for days
and break my daughter's heart;
But back she came, purring her delight.

Molly Shaw

WILD PUSS

Wild puss
Living wild puss
Tough puss
Fighting foe puss
Rough puss, claws extended
See the rat – its life is ended.

Playful puss follows me,
Mews to say 'it's time for tea'.

Loving puss likes a fuss
Snuggles up to each of us.
Scratch my ear, tickle my tum
Or groom my coat – just be my mum.

Sleepy puss
snuggles down
Underneath the eiderdown.
Wild puss called by for tea
And decided to stay with me.

Purrfect!

Barbara Owen

FAT CAT

Our greedy pussy got stuck in the cat flap
And I didn't know what to do.
The dog chased his tail, and the other cats howled,
Oh what a hullabaloo.

When Dad fetched a saw, our Billy cried
'Please don't saw our pussy in two.'
'I'm sawing the DOOR so he'll be free.'
The poor old cat said 'Mew.'

Muriel Berry

FORECAST

If the cat is black,
you'll get the sack.

If it's grey,
you're going away.

If it's white,
you'll score tonight.

If it's a tabby,
your clothes are shabby.

If it's marmalade,
the plane's delayed.

If it's a Persian,
there's a diversion.

If it's a Siamese,
eat a piece of cheese.

If it's a tortoiseshell,
you're doing well.

But if the moggy's pink,
better change your drink.

Margaret Richens

ALGIE

Under laurel leaves, slick
with sunlight, pink nose snuffles
wild strawberries.
Cream petals drift and seagulls
mew overhead.
Summer sport
After a busy evening
listening to cicada orchestras
and dancing with
grasshoppers
through the weeds,
the cat comes home.
He sniffs the bowl of kibble
then looks up, looks
dissatisfied, as if to say,
"dried cat food's
just
not
cricket."

Gwyneth Box

TABLE FOR TWO

A thin hungry tabby creeps out of the shadows,
not one to seek cuddles or curl up on laps.
He knows tourists are suckers for sharing their dinner,
so he loiters round tables in search of some scraps.

The waiters dismiss him as vermin, a nuisance.
They shoo him away with a kick or a hiss,
and the parents shriek about cat fleas or rabies
when their kids try to stroke him or give him a kiss.

But an elderly lady sits under the palm tree.
She is travelling and, of course, eating alone.
She feeds him sardine heads under the table.
He reminds her of Oscar, her moggy back home.

They come to a mutual unspoken agreement.
She's glad of the company, he's glad of the meal.
Tomorrow she will be back on the aircraft,
and he will be scrounging elsewhere; that's the deal.

He demolishes fish bones, licks cream from her fingers.
He rubs round her ankles, she asks him his name.
But belly less empty, he's no need for friendship,
and slinks back to the shadows, the way that he came.

Vivien Hampshire

IT'S A CAT'S LIFE

Hello, my name is Marlon
I'm a fine figured ginger tom
and the important thing about me
is that I'm extremely laaaaazeeeee.

I don't clean out my toilet tray,
I never ever put my toys away,
or forage for food like those feral cats,
oh no, I have a human to do all that.

I devote my life to inward contemplation,
I'm often found in deep meditation
usually on top of the radiator in the hall,
or for variety, I'll sit and stare at a wall.

Years ago, when I was a young catling,
I once had an urge to go mousing.
I spent hours peering at a rodent under the shed
until I realised it was already dead.

Well that experience put paid to hunting activities.
I decided to spend my life in homely captivity,
although who owns who is open to debate
and if I had time I would like to elucidate

but I sense a nap approaching.
Now I don't want you to think I'm gloating
but take a moment to think and reflect,
don't you wish your life was so perfect?

Stephen Beattie

OLLY

For curling, teddy-bear-soft, in a ball
of ginger and lemon fur
to sleep and sleep and sleep;
For always finding the one person
who hates cats
and sitting on their lap;
For stopping, startled, in the middle
of your wash, one leg
stiff in air;
For the ballet dance, points and pirouette,
while you throw and catch
your purple catnip toy;
For occupying more of the duvet
than your fragile weight
can – logically – achieve;
For sneaking titbits from my plate
and smearing sauce
on the pale carpet;
For purring warm
in my ear,
in my heart;

    I give you cream and fish,
    shelter, and more hugs
    than any cat can count.

Alison Chisholm

WINDY WHISKERS

Hunched; paws tucked
like a plucked chicken,
the cat stares from the step.
He risks his fine white whiskers,
defies the wind to ruffle his fur.

He watches the washing
as it leaps in ecstasy,
white shirts waving to one another.
He fluffs out his fur, concentrates
to perfect an accusing look.

I open the door.
He hurtles in,
fast as the wind,
settles in a calm place
and glares. He blames me.

Anne Watson

MY CAT

We met a long time ago, in a room not large or grand.
You sat with patient eyes that gleamed and melted my heart.
You came along with me that day, I took you home,
One small black and white bundle, a hunter and a soul mate.

It was a fair exchange we had, your company for a little food.
You were content with simple things, a touch, a smile, a cuddle.
Golden hours, days that grew into years, times passed with
                                                    happiness.
We made friends, we played, you gave me peace, you showed me
                                                    love.

Ever faithful and gentle, you bring me all these things in
                                                    abundance.
You are a character, one of the family, you ask for nothing, yet
                                                    you give everything.
I love you with an unconditional love, and give it freely with no
                                                    thought of gain.
You are one of my greatest joys. Thank you, dear friend, for
                                                    always being there.

                    Janet Denny

TO THE MANOR BORN

Lord of the window ledge
cat surveys all.
He crouches on haunches,
he curls in a ball.

He spreads soft as butter
(of which he's quite fond)
and dreams of roast pheasant,
poached fish from the pond.

Lord of the lily pool
cat sits to preen.
He watches the ripples
where golden fins gleam.
His whiskers fan forward,
his green eyes turn black.
The dark water shimmers.
His paw shoots out – smack!

Lord of the drawing room
cat sits to pose.
He tucks up his sleek tail,
warms pink ice-cream toes.
His smile is disdainful,
superior, smug.
Don't dare to disturb him
or sit on his rug.

Lord of the manor house
cat surveys all.
He bathes in the sunshine,
eyes birds on the wall.
He dines on fine salmon,
laps cream by the lawn,
then strolls round the terrace
to the manor born.

Celia Gentles

A NON-FESTIVE CAT

I am not a festive cat.
My birthday is invariably forgotten
in the Christmas rush.
I cringe when I recall
they almost named me 'Ginger.'
'Marmalade' has a refined ring
more suited to one
of feline aristocracy.
Preparations are complete.
The room glows robust red,
- tablecloth, napkins, candles, wine,
holly and mistletoe strategically hung,
with paper crackers scattered round the table.
Sausages, plump turkey,
roast potatoes crisped and golden,
have lured my master from the pub.
A blast of cold air greets me.
Snow flakes melt upon the mat.

From my window seat I watch
the progress of these fatuous festivities.
They eat and drink too much,
then quarrel in lopsided cumpled hats.
Tomorrow the house will sleep
while I relax before the fire,
ruminate on delights
of drowsy summer days.

Dylys Osborne

NINE LIVES

She used up the first in a fall from a bough,
landed on paws, safe and sound – miaow!

One day when crossing a fast two-way street,
she missed being roadkill by the skin of her teeth.

While out hunting mice, she nearly drowned;
she fell in a river. Later we found

she'd run up a tree and wouldn't descend.
That time a kind fireman saved my feline friend.

In the fifth life she trapped her head in a tin;
ran round in circles scared out of her skin.

In a close encouter of the pushchair kind,
she ended up with a bruised behind.

Then there were night fights with other cats;
a notch in her ear from one of these spats.

Only two lives left – what does fate plan –
attacked by a rabbit or locked in a van?

At last she feels safe, stretched out by the fire
eating chicken and tuna to her heart's desire.

Margaret Gleave

THE CHESHIRE CAT

Alice had often seen a cat without a grin but never a grin without
a cat

And so I became famous: a grinning Cheshire Cat, springing
from the mind of the poet.
I existed before he brought me forth though
Bubbling through his childhood thoughts into his adult dream.

He and I had known each other for years, always aware, always
there.
Daresbury, Christleton all the Cheshire villages that he knew so
well
I was there, high, aloft in ancient churches
My carved stone eyes holding his blue gaze as the dream began.

Long before I lived in his mind, I had life in the mind of the
mason who carved me.
He had seen me, a flesh and blood lean, blue furred, cat, catching
mice down by the Chester quay
I liked to pull my lips back, prelude to a pounce
But not a grin, unless secretly, once or twice, as I dreamed.

As I silently dreamt, he watched me silently, hand aching to copy
me in stone
And so he did in all the Cheshire churches where he worked, I
was his own private trademark
I waited, soundless, down the long loops of years
A secret to find for those who sensed the dream of a cat.

He found the secret and shared, shared with a solemn child and
then the world
The cat who disappeared bit by bit until only his grin could be
spied.

I am known now. Not for my blue fur, grace or skill.
I am the dream of Lewis Carroll: the Grinning Cheshire Cat.

Mairead Mahon

HE

burnt every whisker when a madcap kitten,
                    made them grow contorted;
split one ear which healed the wrong way over
                    marks him as a pirate;

is black and sleek as tar, careful to keep spotless
                    his white breast and paws;
adapts to train and car, settles in strange cities
                    with innate sang-froid;

walks across the gas stove when a meal is cooking
                    in case there's food to steal,
is a consummate thief; paddles in baths, plays
                    in the washing-up bowl;

stalks intruding May bugs crawling in the kitchen
                    strokes one lightly, teasing;
devours the awkward insect (legs waving, shell crackling)
                    smirks with satisfaction;

swears at gossip sparrows, wrestles with the collie,
                    brings me expiring goldfish;
is of fire and water, of killing and caresses,
                    of guile and of grace.

Peggy Poole

HAUNTING IMAGES

Fog's cold arms swaddle us,
damp licks our cheeks,
ice in winter trees,
a snow image of may blossom.
Glass rods of broom glitter,
colour drained.
Pavements are sealskin
in the neon light.

York Minster's blurred,
an Impressionist painting
in the gaslight.
In the theatre where a nunnery stood
a swirl of grey glides,
ghost of a nun walled up to die
as punishment for love,
a good luck omen now.

Mist wisps the river.
We cobble-clatter to the pub,
enter the lit doorway
to an explosion of chatter.
Light spellbinds.
We clear our fogbound throats.

A black cat,
eyes jewelled,
is circling
invisible legs
on the stairs.

Fay Eagle

OF CATS

Cats are mysterious contradictions.
They hunt, but not always from necessity.
An insinuation through undergrowth,
spies that become assassins,
cats demonstrate co-ordination's joy.

Cats prefer meals at home;
freshly prepared, correct dish, on demand.
(Yesterday's choice is distasteful today.)
Their dainty browsing hides needle teeth.

Cats are lilies-of-the-field,
self-justified glory,
yet their raucous courtship
and coition's outraged indignity
turns beauty to banshee.

Cats are deities, transformed witches
deceptively curled,
purred to dreaming,
in someone's lap.

Cats are never owned,
only borrowed.

Margaret Richens

A CAT CALLED AUDREY

Our Audrey is a clever cat – while dozing on the lawn,
her green eyes are half open; she gives a massive yawn.
But in a flash, she's wide awake, ready to streak across
and catch a careless blackbird seeking worms beneath the grass.

Out Audrey's a stripey tabby, very large and fat.
She goes out on the tiles at night, and hopes to catch a rat.
Sometimes she sneaks through a window to steal a midnight
                                                    meal;
ends up asleep on a neighbour's bed – is this cat for real?

Once she strayed away from home – we really thought we'd
                                                    lost her;
but she turned up days later, covered in mud and plaster.
We cleaned her up as best we could – she really hates the wet.
And just to be on the safe side, we took her to the vet.

She spat at him, he prodded her, gave her a yellow pill,
'In case she's caught a bug,' he said, handing us the bill.
At last she's stopped carousing and spends all nights indoors;
she's given up nocturnal jaunts; the cat flap's locked, secure.

                    Margaret Gleave

ARCHIE

finds a cat-length patch of shade
whisker-wide and hidden
from curious, non-feline eyes.
He dapples into tabby grey.

                    Gwyneth Box

IRIS

Iris is black and lives next door.
Though shy she comes round when she likes;
panthers across the lawn at dawn;
at midday dawdles down the drive
stopping for a word, a touch.
You may not know she's sneaked inside
until a lightweight thunderbolt hurtles
down the stairs and out. Iris reneges:
a step too far, too brave, too strange.

Gail Mosley

THE CAT IN THE WARDROBE

The cat sat in the wardrobe, his eyes shone bold and bright.
He looked out into the room, dimly lit by candlelight.
It is a safe haven here, he thought, among the coats and shoes.
Here he could stay and sleep all day, with nothing much to lose.
He'd played in the garden with spiders and bees.
He'd foraged for titbits, climbed fences and trees.
It had been a good time, he mused, crouching in the gloom,
Until he heard a voice echo his name across the room.
So he lay there motionless, and artfully hedged his bets.
If he didn't move a whisker they'd never find him
To take him to the vet's!

Janet Denny

A MELODRAMATIC SUMMER

I rock in the boat of weather
the sliding sheets of rain,
when glasses tremble together,
cat has forgotten his name.

As thunder gathers to venom,
hills are pulling with strain,
the glasses tremble together,
cat is a prickle of pain.

The hand at the window is lightning,
knives at the door a refrain,
as glasses tremble together –
cat and myself, quite insane.

Cynthia Kitchen

CAT

Prey prowler
Night time howler
Mouse scarer
Kitten carer
Tree climber
Lion mimer
Fish catcher
Arm scratcher
Ouch!

Elizabeth Pope

A KITTEN FOR CHRISTMAS

Day One he sneaked into the fridge,
Enjoyed a turkey tea.
Day Two he knocked the sparkly stars
Down from the Christmas tree.
Day Three he fancied streamers,
Went swinging up and down.
Day Four the tinsel took his eye,
He scattered it around.
Day Five the flashing lights were chewed
And pulled on to the floor.
Day Six the holly ripped apart –
I couldn't take much more.
Day Seven was the fairy's turn,
Her lovely dress so tattered.
Day Eight her wand was rather bent
And baubles bright were shattered.
Day Nine we threatened banishment
If havoc did not stop.
Day Ten he purred and looked so cute
Was pardoned on the spot.
Eleven gone and Christmas cards
Were torn up in a trice.
Twelfth Night, we breathed a sigh at last –
He started chasing mice.

Hilary Tinsley